Y0-DYG-599

BY JESSICA GUNDERSON

PRESIDENT LINCOLN'S KILLER AND THE AMERICA HE LEFT BEHIND

THE ASSASSIN, THE CRIME, AND ITS LASTING BLOW TO FREEDOM AND EQUALITY

COMPASS POINT BOOKS
a capstone imprint

For my parents, who always encouraged my dream of becoming a writer (and who bought me oodles of books about the Civil War when I was a kid) —JG

Special thanks to our consultant, Roger Norton, Founder, Abraham Lincoln Research Site, for his guidance.

Assassins' America is published by Compass Point Books, a Capstone imprint
1710 Roe Crest Drive, North Mankato, Minnesota 56003
www.mycapstone.com

Library of Congress Cataloging-in-Publication Data
Names: Gunderson, Jessica, author.
Title: President Lincoln's killer and the America he left behind : the assassin, the crime, and its lasting blow to freedom and equality / by Jessica Gunderson.
Description: North Mankato, Minnesota : Compass Point Books, 2018. |
Series: Assassins' America | Audience: Ages 9-15.
Identifiers: LCCN 2017042672 (print) | LCCN 2017043547 (ebook) | ISBN 9780756557249 (eBook pdf) | ISBN 9780756557164 (hardcover) | ISBN 9780756557201 (pbk.)
Subjects: LCSH: Lincoln, Abraham, 1809-1865—Assassination—Juvenile literature. | Booth, John Wilkes, 1838-1865—Juvenile literature.
Classification: LCC E457.5 (ebook) | LCC E457.5 .G859 2018 (print) | DDC 973.7092—dc23
LC record available at https://lccn.loc.gov/2017042672

Editorial Credits
Nick Healy, editor; Mackenzie Lopez and Kay Fraser, designers; Svetlana Zhurkin, media researcher; Tori Abraham, production specialist

Printed and bound in the United States of America.
010749S18

TABLE OF CONTENTS

John Wilkes Booth, an actor who became an assassin

CHAPTER 1
LINCOLN'S KILLER

Picture this: President Abraham Lincoln is about to speak from a balcony of the White House. For four long years, the North and South have clashed in bloody battles, leaving hundreds of thousands dead or wounded. But now peace has come at last. It's April 11, 1865. The Civil War is finally over.

Imagine yourself there in the crowd on the White House lawn. You're probably wearing heavy, scratchy clothes — a jacket and a high-buttoned collar, or a long, flouncy dress that's laced so tight it's hard to breathe. The sun has gone down, but the night air is stifling. Maybe you remove your hat and wipe your sweaty forehead, or perhaps you cool yourself with your fold-out fan.

And then you feel a chill at your back. Your whole body grows cold. You turn to find yourself face-to-face with John Wilkes Booth, the well-known stage actor. He's so famous you'd know him anywhere. All the girls your age adore him.

But something about him gives you the creeps. He wears an

angry scowl on his face. His eyes smolder.

With a shudder, you return your attention to the White House balcony. The president has emerged and is talking about bringing the Union back together. "It is unsatisfactory that the black man is not allowed to vote," Lincoln says.

"Now, by God, I'll put him through!" hisses Booth. "That is the last speech he'll ever give."

Put him through? you think. *That means kill him. Did he really just say that?* You stare open-mouthed as Booth whirls around and stomps away.

You try to focus on the president and to hear his piercing voice, but you can't stop thinking about John Wilkes Booth, his murderous stare, and his threatening words. You should call for the police. But you can't, because this is long in the past, after all, and you aren't actually there.

A few days later, President Lincoln would be dead, and Booth — his assassin — would be on the run.

John Wilkes Booth was not what you might expect in a killer. He was handsome, charming, and famous. Think of your favorite movie star. *That's* about how famous he was. And he was young, only 26 years old. He had his whole life ahead of him. Then he made a decision that would change his life — and change the nation forever.

Booth — Johnnie, as many called him — grew up in Maryland, not terribly far from Washington, D.C. He came from a family of actors. His dad, Junius, was a famous actor who had made a name for himself performing Shakespeare's plays. Junius hailed from England and settled on a farm in Bel Air, Maryland, where John

Junius Booth was a noted actor, and his sons followed in his footsteps.

was born in 1838. Maryland was a slaveholding state, and enslaved people tended the farm where he grew up.

Young Johnnie was theatrical from an early age. He loved to tromp through the woods near his home, giving speeches to an audience of trees and birds. He was often late for school. He sometimes got distracted by something on the walk there. He'd follow animals into the woods, making up stories about them. He was definitely more interested in what happened on the way to school than what happened in the classroom.

Booth's two older brothers were actors, like his father, and he wanted to follow in their footsteps. At age 17, John Wilkes Booth got his first chance on stage. He performed in one of Shakespeare's plays in Baltimore. His early performances showed such promise that he was invited to join a Shakespearean acting company. By age 22 he was making $20,000 a year as an actor. That's more than half a million dollars in today's money.

Booth gave bold and memorable performances on stage, and his good looks made him quite popular with the ladies. Often women would crowd around him as he left the theater, sometimes even ripping his clothes. Every day he received fan mail from women who adored him.

What could turn Booth, a beloved and admired actor, into a murderer? Was he A) a cold-blooded killer, B) a racist, C) out for revenge, or D) all of the above?

The answer is most likely D) all of the above. He had a variety of motives, but one thing is certain: He wasn't a madman acting in a moment of rage. His killing of Lincoln was carefully planned out. And he didn't do it alone. He had a web of accomplices.

What led to John Wilkes Booth wanting to kill the president in the first place? In 1860 Abraham Lincoln was elected president. Southern states feared Lincoln would make slavery illegal. Soon several Southern states decided to leave the Union and form their own country, the Confederate States of America. In April 1861 the

Civil War between the Union and Confederacy broke out.

Maryland, Booth's home state, was a border state. Although it was a slave state, it did not join the Confederacy.

But Booth sided with the Confederacy. He was what was called a "Southern sympathizer" — someone who lived in the North but sided with the South. Booth believed that slavery was necessary and right. He also held staunchly racist views. He even wrote, "This country was formed for the white, not the black man."

But he didn't suit up in a Confederate uniform and join the fight. Instead he continued acting, mostly touring Northern cities. At times he spoke out passionately about preserving slavery, calling the South's secession heroic. He wrote: "I will not fight for secession . . . but I will fight heart and soul . . . for justice to the South." He hated President Lincoln and blamed him for the war. He called Lincoln a tyrant who wanted to destroy the South.

As the war went on and the dead piled up, Booth started to feel worthless. Thousands of young men his own age were dying or losing limbs for what they believed in. And all he was doing was acting and talking.

Desperate to do something — anything, it seemed — Booth began meeting with Confederate spies. He went to Montreal, Canada, where agents from the Confederate Secret Service, a network of spies, were meeting. As an actor he was able to cross borders without suspicion and travel through the North and the South. This would make it easy for him to smuggle information to Confederates. No one knows for sure if Booth actually became a spy, although he did claim to have smuggled medicine to the South.

Booth and his co-conspirators first plotted to kidnap President Lincoln.

By mid-1864 the war was turning sharply in the North's favor. Booth was enraged. He stopped acting altogether. He began meeting with Southern sympathizers at Mary Surratt's boardinghouse in Washington, D.C. He started plotting against the North and against President Lincoln.

On March 15, 1865, Booth sat in the back room of Gautier's Restaurant in the capital, gobbling oysters and downing champagne. In front of him was an audience of six men — George Atzerodt, David Herold, Lewis Powell, Samuel Arnold, Michael O'Laughlen, and John Surratt, a Confederate spy. He'd known some of them for years, others for mere months. But they all had one thing in common: They despised the North and Abraham Lincoln.

But this audience wasn't there to watch him act. They weren't even there to eat oysters and drink champagne. They were there to listen to Booth's plan.

Booth might've said something like this: *Listen, fellas. I heard that Lincoln will be attending a play at Campbell Hospital. We'll ambush him on his way home. Kill the driver, capture Lincoln, take him across the river to Virginia, Confederate territory. Then we'll put up a ransom. Lincoln in exchange for all Confederate prisoners.*

The plan seemed like it could work. Back then there was no Secret Service to protect the president. Lincoln usually traveled without guards. Booth and his conspirators figured they could easily overtake Lincoln's carriage. And if the ransom demand was met, Booth thought, the released prisoners would rejoin the Confederate Army. The South would regain military strength.

But Lincoln changed his mind and didn't go to Campbell Hospital. Surratt later said the group had approached a carriage in hopes of carrying out their plan two days after the restaurant meeting. The carriage held Secretary of the Treasury Salmon Chase, not Lincoln. Chase's carriage continued on, and Booth's plan failed.

But he was determined to try again. Three weeks later, on April 9, Confederate General Robert E. Lee surrendered to Union General Ulysses S. Grant. Although a few smaller armies still battled, the war was essentially over. The South had lost.

The South's surrender sent Booth into a rage. The Southern cause, which he'd become so passionate about, was now a lost cause. But maybe he could do something about it. Maybe the

Robert E. Lee surrendered to Ulysses S. Grant at Appomattox Court House in Virginia, April 9, 1865.

South could rise again.

All across Washington, D.C., crowds celebrated the end of the war. Booth didn't celebrate. He wandered the city in a dejected state. He clung to hope. Maybe the few remaining Confederate armies would refuse to surrender.

On April 11 Booth was in the crowd outside the White House as Lincoln spoke about the end of the war and giving freed slaves full citizenship. Booth made up his mind, right then and there, that Lincoln had to die. And he would be the one to kill him.

Abraham Lincoln as a young man

CHAPTER 2
LINCOLN'S STORY

Abraham Lincoln, the sixteenth president of the United States, is widely considered one of America's greatest presidents. He led the country through the Civil War with determination to keep the United States together and to defeat those who would break it apart. He declared that all slaves would be free, and with the war won, he spoke of binding up wounds. He was determined to repair the country and rebuild the South. He dreamed of brighter days until John Wilkes Booth shot him dead.

But long before all that, he was just a kid living a hardscrabble life in southern Indiana. He was born in 1809 in a one-room log cabin in Kentucky. Seven years later the Lincolns moved to Indiana, where Abe spent most of his childhood years. His life wasn't exactly easy. His mother died when he was nine. And he didn't get along with his father, Thomas. Abe liked to spend his time reading, and his dad thought he was lazy. Imagine! Calling

Abe Lincoln — a kid who would eventually become president — lazy!

Abe had very little formal education. He liked school, but since the Lincolns were poor, he had to work to help support the family. He was mostly self-taught. He read anything he could find, often reading books over and over.

When Abe was 21, his family moved to Illinois. He joined them, although he didn't live with them for long. He worked a variety of jobs: boatman, storekeeper, militiaman, postmaster. He taught himself law and eventually became a lawyer. His law career led him on a path to the presidency.

Perhaps you've heard the story of "Honest Abe." The one where he walks 5 miles, uphill both ways, to return a nickel? Or was it 10 miles in a blizzard to return a library book? That story has many versions, but there is truth behind the legend. When he was working as a store clerk, Abe realized he hadn't given a customer the right amount of change. So he closed the store and walked several miles to return the correct change to the customer.

Honesty was only one of Lincoln's finer qualities. He was driven. He was intelligent. (Some historians think he was the smartest president in U.S. history.) He was charming and had a great sense of humor. He loved to tell jokes. His laughter helped lighten the mood and drew people to him.

But beneath the jokes, Lincoln struggled with depression and grief. Life had not been easy on his family. Long before Lincoln's presidency, his son Edward died at a young age in 1850. While in the White House, Lincoln's son Willie died in 1862 at age 11. The president had jarring mood swings. One minute he'd be laughing,

Willie Lincoln died of typhoid fever less than a year after his family moved into the White House.

and the next he'd be in despair. He called himself "the loneliest man in the world."

When Lincoln was running for president in 1860, the story of "Honest Abe" was used in campaign ads. Lincoln (Republican) ran against three top contenders: Stephen Douglas (Northern Democrat), John C. Breckinridge (Southern Democrat), and John Bell (Constitutional Unionist).

Abraham Lincoln frightened Southern slave owners. He was against the spread of slavery. In other words, he didn't want slavery to be legal in newly formed states and territories in the West. Southerners felt their way of life was under attack. So when Lincoln easily won the election, eight Southern states quickly seceded, or separated, from the United States to form their own country, the Confederate States of America. Four more states would eventually join them.

Lincoln wanted more than anything to keep the United States together. He felt secession was illegal according to the U.S. Constitution. Basically, he begged the South to come back. During his inauguration speech in March 1861, Lincoln stated that he would not interfere with slavery that already existed in the South, as long as the Confederate States rejoined the Union. But the Confederate leaders refused.

So Lincoln began his presidency with a country that was crumbling at his feet. Then Confederates fired on Union-held Fort Sumter in Charleston, South Carolina. That was the first battle of the long, grisly Civil War, which killed more than 600,000 and left many Southern cities in ruins.

Abraham Lincoln received about 40 percent of the popular vote and defeated three other candidates for the presidency in 1860.

Lincoln is one of the most popular presidents today, but during his presidency, he was sharply criticized. He had many political enemies, some within his own party. Lincoln had to make many tough decisions throughout the war, such as holding Confederate sympathizers in prison without trial. Many believed his actions went against Americans' rights and freedoms. But Lincoln believed these harsh actions were necessary in war times.

Lincoln is often called the Great Emancipator for his role in freeing slaves. But that wasn't always his goal. When he began his presidency, he wanted only to keep the Union together. He despised slavery, but he believed it was legal under the Constitution. He was willing to let the South hold on to slavery in order to save the nation.

Divided opinions over the future of slavery even reached into the president's family. Strange as it may seem now, Lincoln's wife came from a wealthy slaveholding family from Kentucky. Some of Mary Todd Lincoln's relatives even fought for the Confederacy.

By 1862, though, Lincoln's views on slavery had changed. He made up his mind to emancipate (or free) the slaves. With his famous Emancipation Proclamation on January 1, 1863, Lincoln declared slavery illegal in rebellious states. This raised the stakes for the Confederates: win the war or slavery dies. The proclamation also raised the stakes for Union troops. They were no longer fighting only to preserve the Union. They were fighting for human freedom. About the Emancipation Proclamation, Lincoln said, "If my name ever goes into history, it will be for this act."

By the war's end, Lincoln's views on slavery and African-American rights would move even further from where he stood before arriving in the White House. He would come to believe that African Americans should have equal rights.

As the war dragged on, Abraham Lincoln was haunted by all the death and destruction. He spent hours writing letters to dead soldiers' families, expressing his grief. The distress took a toll on his body. His face was now lined with wrinkles. The painter Francis Carpenter described him as having "great black rings under his eyes, such a picture of the effects of sorrow."

Despite his many critics and enemies, Lincoln never feared for his life. From his very first days in office, Lincoln began receiving death threats. He kept the most threatening letters in a cubbyhole of his desk. But he treated the threats lightly. He didn't think anyone would actually kill him. Even after a bullet whizzed by his head while he was riding a horse one summer night, he shrugged the threats off.

Lincoln was a great lover of theater and was also a fan of John Wilkes Booth. He saw Booth star in the play *The Marble Heart* in 1863. He sent invitations to Booth, asking him to visit the White House. But Booth never responded to the invitations. Little did Lincoln know that one day Booth would respond, and he would meet Lincoln's kindness with violence.

A depiction of the slaughter of antislavery settlers in Kansas

CHAPTER 3
TROUBLED TIMES

Years before Lincoln's election, an armed posse of 800 proslavery men descended upon Lawrence, Kansas. The date was May 21, 1856. The mob ransacked the newspaper offices, smashed the printing press, and burned papers and books. The men then ransacked and set fire to the town's hotel. As flames rose from the hotel, the mob marched through the streets, pillaging and burning all buildings that lay in their path. By nightfall the town was in smoldering ruins.

A few days later, the abolitionist John Brown and a group of his antislavery followers set out for revenge. They waited until night fell. Then they marched to the homes of five proslavery settlers, dragged them from their beds, and hacked them to death. This became known as the Pottawatomie Creek Massacre.

These skirmishes, along with others, caused the territory to become known as Bleeding Kansas. So what did Bleeding Kansas, far away on the western frontier, have to do with the Civil War? Bleeding Kansas was part of a fight over slave states and free states. Tensions had been brewing for decades over the issue of free states, slave states, and whether slavery would grow into new territories. More and more people were settling the west. Settlers from the South brought their slaves with them. This led to a question: Should western territories and newly admitted states allow slavery?

After years of rising tension, a compromise was reached in Washington, D.C. The Compromise of 1850 stated, in short, that citizens of territories and states should decide for themselves whether slavery should be legal. The compromise brought a sense of relief to the American people. Many Americans feared that the slavery issue would break the nation apart, and the compromise seemed to calm these fears (or at least push the slavery issue aside).

The Kansas-Nebraska Act of 1854 echoed the Compromise of 1850. White settlers could choose by popular vote whether Kansas and Nebraska would be free or slave states. The territory of Kansas bordered Missouri, a slave state. Determined abolitionists poured into Kansas, hoping to make it a free state. Proslavery settlers also poured into the area, hoping to make it a slave state. Violence erupted as proslavery and antislavery factions attacked each other. From 1854 to 1861, 56 people died in Bleeding Kansas conflicts. Although the Civil War didn't officially begin until 1861, you could say Kansas saw the first blood spilled of the Civil War.

For many in the South, slavery was an important thread in the fabric of their lives. The first slaves were brought to American colonies in 1619, long before the United States became a nation.

Slavery quickly spread throughout the colonies. More than 7 million slaves were brought from Africa in the 18th century. Slaves mostly worked on large farms and plantations along the Southern coast, toiling on tobacco, indigo, and rice plantations. In 1793 the invention of the cotton gin allowed for the growing of cotton in the South.

Slavery was not as widespread in the Northern states, and one by one Northern states moved to ban slavery within their borders. By 1804 slavery was illegal in all Northern states. In 1808 the United States outlawed importing slaves from Africa. However, anyone born into slavery was a slave for life and could be bought or sold at any time.

The 1830s and 1840s saw the rise of the abolitionist movement — a movement to make slavery illegal in the United States. Abolitionists helped slaves escape through the Underground Railroad, a network of safe houses. Abolitionists also vowed to keep any new states from becoming slave states.

Those forces led to Bleeding Kansas and abolitionist John Brown. After the Pottawatomie Creek Massacre, Brown returned east and began thinking of a way to free slaves in Virginia. The best way to do it, he thought, was to arm slaves with weapons so they could rise up against their owners. In October 1859, Brown and 21 other men raided Harpers Ferry, an arsenal of federal weapons. They planned to steal weapons for the slave uprising, but their plan failed. John Brown was captured, put on trial, and sentenced to death for treason. Before his hanging, Brown had to be heavily guarded in case he tried to escape. Volunteers lined up to guard him. Following along with some of those volunteers was

John Brown crusaded against slavery and used violence to advance his cause.

the young actor John Wilkes Booth.

Booth both hated and admired John Brown. He didn't like what Brown stood for — the ending of slavery. But he admired that Brown had taken action for what he believed in. Some say Brown's hanging was the spark that led to John Wilkes Booth's assassination plan.

Where did Abraham Lincoln stand while all of this transpired? Lincoln was against the spread of slavery to new states and territories. As an individual, he believed slavery was wrong. But as a lawyer and politician, he believed that slavery was protected by the U.S. Constitution in the states where it already existed.

Even so, Lincoln's election in November 1860 was the final straw for many in the South. Lincoln hadn't carried a single Southern state. Southerners felt they were losing power in Washington, D.C. The loss of this power would mean that they couldn't carry out proslavery agendas. Seven states — South Carolina, Mississippi, Florida, Alabama, Georgia, Louisiana, and Texas — seceded from the Union. They established their own government under the Confederate States of America in February 1861, before Lincoln even officially took office. The Confederates chose Jefferson Davis to be their president.

The Confederacy seized Union forts throughout the South. But Union troops remained at Fort Sumter, in Charleston Harbor, South Carolina. On the morning of April 12, 1861, Confederate forces bombarded Fort Sumter. Eventually Union forces

Jefferson Davis, president of the Confederate States, had earlier represented Mississippi in the U.S. Congress.

surrendered. The Battle of Fort Sumter signaled the beginning of the Civil War. After Sumter, four more states — Arkansas, North Carolina, Tennessee, and Virginia — joined the Confederacy.

No one realized what a long and violent conflict awaited the country. Many people, including President Lincoln, thought the North would easily quash the South's rebellion. In July Union troops entered Virginia with the hopes of taking the Confederate capital of Richmond. It was a beautiful day, and many residents of Washington, D.C., decided to go watch the battle. They packed carriages with picnic lunches and set off to the battle site along the Bull Run River near Manassas Junction. Men and women perched atop a hill to watch the battle, almost as if they were attending a sporting event.

At first it seemed the Union would win. But the Confederates had amassed a large number of troops. A late afternoon Confederate charge sent the Union troops into a panicked retreat. Chaos erupted as troops and civilians scrambled away, back toward the capital.

With the First Battle of Bull Run, it was apparent that the war would not end quickly and would not be easily won. Confederate forces won significant victories in the first two years of the war. It seemed that the Union, which Lincoln had vowed to preserve, would fall.

The dead from both sides lay scattered across battlefields. The wounded filled hospitals. Prisoners of war filled Confederate and Union prisons. Disease and illness spread through army camps. As the war continued without an end in sight, many people — Northerners and Southerners alike — blamed President Lincoln.

The 54th Massachusetts Infantry Regiment in combat at Fort Wagner in South Carolina, where the African American regiment made a famous charge

Almost every family was affected by the war. Many men joined up or were drafted. Women were left to care for the family, often having to find jobs or tend farmland. Poor families were more affected by the war than the rich. In the North, men could avoid the draft by paying a $300 fee. In the South, men who owned at least 20 slaves didn't have to fight. In fact, many Confederate soldiers didn't even own slaves.

Most Civil War battles were fought in the South. Women and

children witnessed war firsthand, right on their doorsteps.

It's important to note that not all Southerners supported the Confederacy. "Unionists" were people living in Confederate states who opposed secession. And not all Northerners wanted a war to preserve the Union. Anti-war Northerners were called "Copperheads." Southern sympathizers, like John Wilkes Booth, were those who lived in the North but supported the Southern cause. Also, not every slave state joined the Confederacy. The border states of Maryland, Delaware, West Virginia, Kentucky, and Missouri were slave states but remained in the Union.

On January 1, 1863, Lincoln took a stand against slavery with the Emancipation Proclamation. He announced that the goal of

Lincoln (seen without a hat near the center at the front of the group facing the camera) delivers his brief but historic address at the dedication of the cemetery at Gettysburg, Pennsylvania.

the war was not just to preserve the Union. Now the goal was also to eliminate slavery in the South.

Before the Emancipation Proclamation, free African Americans couldn't officially join the Union Army. But in the South, slaves were *forced* to support the war effort. They built forts and worked in armories and hospitals. The efforts of the slaves were helping the Confederacy — and continuing their enslavement.

After the Proclamation, African Americans could legally join the Union Army. Frederick Douglass, an abolitionist leader who'd escaped from slavery, urged his fellow African Americans to enlist. Many of them did. About 190,000 African Americans fought for the Union by the end of the war.

In July 1863 a Union victory at the Battle of Gettysburg marked a major turning point in the war. Union victories now stacked up against Confederate victories. But Lincoln still faced scrutiny and opposition. In 1864 some Republican leaders believed Lincoln shouldn't even run for a second term. They felt he would surely lose to the Democratic candidate, General George B. McClellan. A faction of the Democratic Party wanted to negotiate for peace with the Confederacy, and whether or how McClellan might have continued the war was uncertain.

By September, though, the war looked like it was finally nearing the end. Union General William Tecumseh Sherman captured Atlanta, Georgia, in the heart of the South. It was a major victory. Lincoln won reelection.

With the end of war in sight, Lincoln was faced with the task of Reconstruction — rebuilding the nation and figuring out how to re-admit the Confederate states into the Union. Some members of his administration wanted the South to be punished harshly. Lincoln wanted mercy for the South. In his Second Inaugural Address, he said he wanted to rebuild the nation "with malice toward none, with charity for all."

But Abraham Lincoln was never able to put his plan for Reconstruction into effect. John Wilkes Booth would change the path of history with a single bullet.

Ford's Theatre in 1865

CHAPTER 4
BOOTH'S CRIME

John Wilkes Booth stopped by Ford's Theatre in Washington, D.C., on April 14, 1865. He was there to get his mail. But while there, he learned something that caused his pulse to quicken and his mind to race. That very night President Lincoln would be attending the play *Our American Cousin* at the theater. General Grant would be there with him.

What luck! This was Booth's chance. He knew the theater inside and out. He'd performed there many times. He knew exactly where the president would be sitting — the Presidential Box in the balcony. He knew the play line by line too. While the audience was laughing uproariously at a funny line, Booth could creep into the Presidential Box, kill the president and General Grant, and escape amidst the chaos.

But his idea went even further. What if he took out not only Lincoln and Grant, but also Vice President Andrew Johnson and

Lincoln and his cabinet, which included others whom Booth plotted to kill

Secretary of State William Seward? With its top leaders dead, the government would collapse. The Union would collapse, he imagined. The South could rise again!

And Booth had a team of conspirators to help him carry out the plan.

Booth scurried from the theater. He had a lot to do to put his plan in place. First he went to a livery stable and secured a getaway horse. Booth knew he would need to escape Washington after the assassination. He would head south. Once he crossed into Virginia, a Confederate state, he'd be safe, he figured.

He visited his friend Mary Surratt and told her to have weapons ready at her tavern along their escape route. (No one knows if he told her of the assassination plot. Remember that. It will be important later.)

Booth headed to a tavern and had a drink. Then he wrote a letter to a newspaper, the *National Intelligencer*. In the letter, he described that his plans had changed from kidnapping to assassinating Lincoln. He signed his name along with the names of David Herold, Lewis Powell, and George Atzerodt. He gave the letter to a friend, John Mathews, and told him to deliver it the next day.

Why on earth would Booth send a letter to a newspaper confessing his crime? And before it even happened? Here's why: Booth was proud of his plan. He thought others would be proud of him too. He thought he would be revered. He figured he'd be a hero for saving the nation from the "tyrant" Abraham Lincoln. That's not quite what happened.

While Booth was giving his letter to Mathews, he glimpsed a carriage passing by. Inside was General Grant. The carriage was headed toward the train station. He realized Grant was not going to be attending the theater that night. But he was still determined to kill Lincoln.

Booth went back to Ford's to make some final preparations. The Presidential Box was a private balcony seat that had two doors, an outer door and an inner door. Booth may have carved a hole in the frame of the outer door — or perhaps the hole was already there. Either way, he planned to wedge in a wooden stick, barring the door from the inside. After slipping into the box, he would put the makeshift lock in place. Anyone who suspected that something was wrong would have to break down the door. By then, Booth figured, the deed would be done.

At points throughout the day, Booth met with his

accomplices — Lewis Powell, David Herold, and George Atzerodt. Who were these guys, and what tasks did Booth give them?

Lewis Powell (alias Lewis Payne) was a Confederate soldier who'd been wounded and captured at the Battle of Gettysburg. He escaped a Union hospital and went on to serve in a Confederate cavalry unit called Mosby's Regiment. He left the unit and took an oath of allegiance to the Union. He likely took this oath so he could be a Confederate spy. Booth told him to go to Secretary Seward's house that evening at 10:15 p.m. Seward was recovering from a carriage accident, so would be in his bed. Powell was told to pretend he was there to deliver medicine — and to kill Seward once inside.

David Herold was an avid hunter and pharmacist's assistant. His knowledge of backwoods would make him helpful in the assassins' getaway from the capital. Booth gave him an assignment. He was to wait for Powell outside Seward's house. Together they were to leave the city and meet the rest of the group at Soper's Hill, Maryland.

George Atzerodt was a German immigrant who owned a carriage repair business in Maryland. At Booth's order, he was staying at the Kirkwood House in Washington, D.C. This is where Vice President Johnson was also staying. Booth told Atzerodt to go to Johnson's room around 10 o'clock that night — and to kill him.

The accomplices had one final meeting that evening. The stage was set. Each accomplice knew his role. By the end of the night, the top leaders of the U.S. government would be dead. If all went according to plan, that is.

David Herold

Meanwhile, Abraham Lincoln woke that morning having no inkling that day would be his last. He was in jolly spirits. The war was over. A new dawn was breaking for the United States. And he, Lincoln, would lead the country from darkness to light.

Lincoln met with his cabinet that morning. He told his advisers that he hoped to be lenient with the South. Secretary of War Edwin Stanton disagreed. He thought the South should be punished. General Grant was also at the meeting. He told Lincoln he wouldn't be able to go to the play with him that night. Mary Lincoln invited Major Henry Rathbone and his fiancée, Clara Harris, instead.

In the afternoon Lincoln and his wife took a carriage ride. Mary complained of a headache and told her husband they should stay home that night. But Lincoln insisted on going to Ford's Theatre.

Around 8 p.m. the President and First Lady set off for the theater, picking up Henry Rathbone and Clara Harris on the way. They were late. The play was already in progress. When the group stepped into the theater, the actress on stage spotted Lincoln. She stopped performing and began clapping. Soon the entire crowd was giving Lincoln a standing ovation as he took his seat in the Presidential Box.

The play resumed, and Lincoln grabbed his wife's hand. After four long years of war, he was feeling at peace.

★ ★ ★

Just after 9:30 p.m., Booth galloped on his rented horse

to the alley behind Ford's Theatre. He leapt off the horse and threw the reins to a theater worker. "Hold my horse for a bit," he told the worker. "I'll be back." Then he slipped in the back door and listened. The play had begun. He knew the play well, and he knew it would be another hour until the actor Harry Hawk spoke the humorous line that would make the audience erupt in laughter, drowning out the gunshot.

He crept beneath the stage and went out the side door. He could use a drink to calm his nerves. He headed next door to Taltavul's Saloon and ordered whiskey. The clock was ticking. It was almost time.

Booth strode through the front door of the theater, greeted the ticket clerk, and made his way upstairs to the balcony. A few theatergoers recognized him, whispering as he passed. He paid his fans no attention. He was on a mission.

Only one man — the President's footman Charles Forbes — stood outside the door to the Presidential Box. Booth showed him his calling card. Forbes nodded and let him in.

Quickly and quietly Booth slid the stick of wood into place to bar the door. He could hear the actors' lines from the stage. Quietly he opened the second door. Then he heard his cue: "Don't know the manners of good society, eh? Well, I guess I know enough to turn you inside out, old gal; you sockdologizing old man-trap!"

The audience exploded with laughter. Booth's gun exploded too. A single shot slammed into the back of Lincoln's head.

The gunshot echoed throughout the theater. Gun smoke drifted into the air. Major Rathbone leapt from his seat and tried

Lincoln, his wife, and their guests had turned their attention to the stage when Booth entered the Presidential Box. They didn't notice him until he fired his pistol.

to tackle Booth. In the scuffle the gun clattered to the floor. But Booth had another weapon — his knife. He slashed Rathbone in the arm. Rathbone staggered back. Blood from his wound sprayed the box.

Booth shouted grandly as he jumped to the stage below. He said, "Sic Semper Tyrannis!" — meaning "Thus always to tyrants!" His left ankle snagged on one of the banners on the balcony, and he fell awkwardly. The crowd buzzed with confusion. What was the famous John Wilkes Booth doing on stage? Was this part of the play? Why was Mary Lincoln screaming, "Stop that man!"?

Before anyone could realize President Lincoln had just been shot, Booth scurried, limping, out the back door and hurdled onto his horse. Then he raced away into the night.

Around the same time, Lewis Powell and David Herold approached Secretary Seward's home, according to most histories of the evening. Powell banged on the door while Herold waited in the shadows. "I'm here to deliver medicine to the secretary," Powell told the servant who opened the door. When the servant refused to let him in, Powell pushed his way through the door and ran up the stairs. Two of Seward's sons tried to stop him, but Powell bludgeoned one son with his gun and stabbed the other with his dagger.

He then burst through Secretary Seward's door, pounced upon him, and stabbed him three times. Seward's nurse tried to pull Powell off, but he stabbed the nurse too. Then Powell ran down the stairs, slashing two more who tried to stop him. He dashed out into the night, leaving the bloody scene behind, ready to climb on the horse and take off out of town. But the horse was not there — nor was David Herold.

Herold, spooked by the screams coming from inside the house, had galloped away, leaving Powell behind.

Powell wandered and hid himself in the city for days. All roads out of Washington, D.C., were blocked. He was stuck there with no hope of reconnecting with Booth and the others.

And what of George Atzerodt's attempts to kill Vice President Johnson? Before the planned time of assassination, Atzerodt was beginning to get cold feet. He went to a bar to get a drink. But he didn't stop at just one drink. He drank and drank. Maybe he forgot what he was supposed to do. Or maybe he lost his courage. Or perhaps he was too drunk to do it. In any case, he went back to his room and fell asleep. He made no attempt whatsoever to kill Johnson. Atzerodt would say later that he had been part of the failed kidnapping plan but had never agreed to assassinate Johnson.

★ ★ ★

Back at Ford's Theatre, Dr. Charles Leale was the first to come to Lincoln's aid. The president was still breathing. His head was cradled in his wife's lap as she hunched over him, weeping. Dr. Leale examined him, finding that the bullet was lodged in the president's skull. There was no saving him. Leale then uttered the dreaded words: "His wound is mortal."

Lincoln was carried across the street to the Petersen Boarding House, where he could die in peace. A sobbing Mary and several solemn cabinet members and doctors surrounded him, watching him struggle to live. At 7:22 the next morning, President Abraham Lincoln breathed his last.

And his killer, John Wilkes Booth, was still on the loose.

Abraham Lincoln

SURRAT.   BOOTH.   HAROLD.

War Department, Washington, April 20, 1865,

$100,000 REWARD!

THE MURDERER

Of our late beloved President, Abraham Lincoln,

IS STILL AT LARGE.

$50,000 REWARD

Will be paid by this Department for his apprehension, in addition to any reward offered by Municipal Authorities or State Executives.

$25,000 REWARD

Will be paid for the apprehension of JOHN H. SURRATT, one of Booth's Accomplices.

$25,000 REWARD

Will be paid for the apprehension of David C. Harold, another of Booth's accomplices.

LIBERAL REWARDS will be paid for any information that shall conduce to the arrest of either of the above-named criminals, or their accomplices.

All persons harboring or secreting the said persons, or either of them, or aiding or assisting their concealment or escape, will be treated as accomplices in the murder of the President and the attempted assassination of the Secretary of State, and shall be subject to trial before a Military Commission and the punishment of DEATH.

Let the stain of innocent blood be removed from the land by the arrest and punishment of the murderers.

All good citizens are exhorted to aid public justice on this occasion. Every man should consider his own conscience charged with this solemn duty, and rest neither night nor day until it be accomplished.

EDWIN M. STANTON, Secretary of War.

DESCRIPTIONS.—BOOTH is Five Feet 7 or 8 inches high, slender build, high forehead, black hair, black eyes, and wears a heavy black moustache.

JOHN H. SURRAT is about 5 feet, 9 inches. Hair rather thin and dark ; eyes rather light ; no beard. Would weigh 145 or 150 pounds. Complexion rather pale and clear, with color in his cheeks. Wore light clothes of fine quality. Shoulders square ; cheek bones rather prominent ; chin narrow ; ears projecting at the top ; forehead rather low and square, but broad. Parts his hair on the right side ; neck rather long. His lips are firmly set. A slim man.

DAVID C. HAROLD is five feet six inches high, hair dark, eyes dark, eyebrows rather heavy, full face, nose short, hand short and fleshy, feet small, instep high, round bodied, naturally quick and active, slightly closes his eyes when looking at a person.

NOTICE.—In addition to the above, State and other authorities have offered rewards amounting to almost one hundred thousand dollars, making an aggregate of about TWO HUNDRED THOUSAND DOLLARS.

Rewards were offered for Booth and his accomplices when they were on the run.

CHAPTER 5
THE AFTERMATH

Panic gripped Washington, D.C. President Lincoln was dead. Secretary of State William Seward had narrowly survived a gruesome attack. Clearly, a conspiracy was afoot. Who was next?

Members of Congress and Lincoln's cabinet huddled at their homes, afraid to leave. What if they were targets? No one knew how far the conspiracy spread. And no one knew who was behind the conspiracy. People wondered if the Confederates had plotted with Booth to kill Lincoln. They wondered if war would begin again.

In the days following the assassination, angry mobs stormed prisons holding Confederate soldiers. Any man who looked even a little bit like Booth was apprehended and questioned. Southern sympathizers were attacked. Some historians believe that nearly 200 Southern sympathizers were killed to avenge Lincoln's death.

But along with the rage came a deep sorrow. Black flags

draped homes and businesses. Any parades or parties celebrating the end of the war were canceled.

African Americans feared that the death of Lincoln meant the death of the Emancipation Proclamation. Many wondered whether they'd be thrown back into slavery.

Not everyone mourned Lincoln, though. Some newspapers in the South celebrated his death. Some Northerners did too. They blamed him for the war that had wrecked their country. But many people on both sides grieved and worried. No one knew how the nation would fare without Lincoln at the helm.

The night of the assassination, Secretary of War Edwin Stanton organized a manhunt to catch John Wilkes Booth and his accomplices. Booth's room was raided. One by one, suspects were rounded up. On April 17 Lewis Powell, after days of wandering around and sleeping in a cemetery, was arrested when he found his way to Mary Surratt's boardinghouse. Mary Surratt, Michael O'Laughlen, Samuel Arnold, and Ned Spangler (a stagehand at Ford's Theatre) were also arrested. A few days later, authorities found George Atzerodt hiding at his cousin's house. Dr. Samuel Mudd was arrested after housing Booth and David Herold for a night.

But John Wilkes Booth was still nowhere to be found. A massive search effort covered the countryside, from Washington, D.C., to Virginia, the largest manhunt the nation had ever known. Search parties fed off tips and often narrowly missed Booth and Herold.

After the assassination Booth and Herold met up at Soper's Hill. When Powell and Atzerodt didn't show, they continued on.

John Wilkes Booth's final hiding spot was in a barn in Virginia, where troops set the building ablaze, shot Booth, and dragged him out.

For 12 days, Booth and Herold stayed on the run, hiding in the woods, making their way across swampland, engaging the help of known Confederates, and wearing disguises and pretending to be soldiers returning from the war. All the while Booth read reports of his deed. Expecting to be hailed a hero, he was dismayed at being called a coward by the newspapers. Afraid, cold, hungry, and dirty, he railed against his fate: "I struck boldly and not as the papers say," he wrote in his diary. "Our country owed all her troubles to him . . . After being hunted like a dog . . . I am here in despair."

On April 26 Booth and Herold were staying in the Garrett family barn in Virginia. In the wee morning hours, federal

The scene moments before several of Booth's accomplices where hanged for their crimes

authorities surrounded the barn, demanding Booth emerge. He refused. So the authorities set fire to the barn, hoping to flush them out. Herold surrendered, but Booth still refused. He swung open the barn door and, silhouetted by flames, raised his gun. Fearing Booth would fire, a young soldier named Boston Corbett shot him. Booth collapsed and was dragged out. He died soon thereafter, murmuring, "Tell Mother I die for my country."

The other conspirators were put on trial. George Atzerodt, Lewis Powell, David Herold, and Mary Surratt were sentenced to death. But wait . . . why was Mary Surratt sentenced to die? Did she really have much to do with the assassination? Did she even know about the assassination plot? Historians are unsure of the extent of her role and her knowledge of events. In court prosecutors maintained that her boardinghouse was the nest where the plot was hatched. Mary claimed she had nothing to do with the assassination and that she was innocent. But still, she was hanged along with the others. Mary Surratt was the very first woman to be executed by the U.S. government.

After his death Lincoln's body was placed on a funeral train to carry him from Washington, D.C., to his final resting place of Springfield, Illinois. The train retraced the route Lincoln had traveled back in 1861 to take office, a distance of 1,654 miles. Mourners lined the tracks to bid goodbye to the president. The

The train carrying President Lincoln's casket drew large crowds as it traveled from Washington, D.C., to Illinois.

funeral procession made several stops in various cities. In New York City, thousands gathered as the horse-drawn hearse moved through the streets. From a high window, a little boy leaned out to watch the funeral procession. The boy was Theodore "Teddy" Roosevelt. Years later Teddy would become president after the assassination of President William McKinley.

Thanks perhaps to George Atzerodt's drunken cowardice, Vice President Andrew Johnson was very much alive and able to take on the role of president. But Johnson had none of Lincoln's political knowledge and skill. And worse, he didn't believe in equal rights for African Americans.

In the years following Lincoln's death, the nation set about reconstructing the South and re-admitting Confederate states into the Union. Johnson took control of Reconstruction, and historians far and wide believe he botched it.

At first Radical Republicans thought Johnson would be tough on the South. Secretary of War Edwin Stanton wanted Confederate leaders punished. But instead, Johnson wanted to deal with them lightly. Johnson himself was a Southerner, hailing from North Carolina and Tennessee. He came from a background of poverty, and he felt resentment against wealthy white planters in the South. So, rather than holding all Southern whites accountable for secession, he pardoned all whites except for wealthy planters and Confederate leaders. With this pardon, whites regained their property and political rights.

Consider this for a moment: white Southerners regaining their land. How did this affect the newly freed slaves? Some Republican leaders felt the slaves should be given land as reparation —

President Andrew Johnson

in other words, as compensation for the hardship of slavery. Republican leaders thought slaves should be given the land they had worked on. But when Johnson gave the land back to previous white owners instead, many newly freed slaves had no choice but to work for white landowners. Most African Americans had no other way to make a living. In effect this led to a system of white landownership and black servitude, a system that was hardly different from slavery.

Stanton and other Radical Republicans also wanted the federal government to have a strong presence in the South. But Johnson felt otherwise. He permitted states to form their own local governments, allowing them to eventually create their own laws. This led to "black codes." Black codes took away civil liberties for African Americans in the South. These laws restricted the rights of African Americans to vote, own property, and own guns. Black codes also punished any African Americans who were out of work, making them criminals. For the next 100 years, African Americans in the South would not have the same legal rights as whites. African Americans had to go to different schools, eat at different restaurants, and drink from different water fountains. During Reconstruction the Ku Klux Klan emerged as a hate group that launched violent acts against African Americans and other groups. Racism remained strong in the South, stoked by Johnson's failed Reconstruction policies.

In the 1950s African Americans rose up against segregation in the Civil Rights Movement. You may have heard of Rosa Parks. In 1955 Parks refused to give up her seat to a white man in Montgomery, Alabama. This led to a city-wide bus boycott.

Rosa Parks refused to give up her seat on a city bus in Montgomery, Alabama.

Leading the boycott was a young minister named Dr. Martin Luther King Jr. He went on to become the most famous and inspiring leader of the Civil Rights Movement.

At long last the Civil Rights Movement resulted in changed laws for African Americans in the South. A different President Johnson — Lyndon B. Johnson — signed the Civil Rights Act of 1964 and the Voting Rights Act of 1965. (Coincidentally, President Lyndon B. Johnson became president after a presidential assassination too — the assassination of John F. Kennedy.) These acts protected equal rights for African Americans.

So, what might have happened if John Wilkes Booth hadn't gone to Ford's Theatre that fateful morning to pick up his mail? Or if his bullet missed its mark? What would Reconstruction have been like under President Lincoln? Would we even know the names of Martin Luther King Jr. or Rosa Parks? If Lincoln had lived, would racial segregation in the South have existed for so long? Would we, perhaps, have had an African-American president long before Barack Obama?

No one knows the answer to these questions, but many historians have speculated what America would have been like if Lincoln lived.

Lincoln didn't live long enough to create a solid plan for Reconstruction, but he definitely had some ideas in mind. He wanted equal citizenship and voting rights for African Americans. He wanted a "practical system by which the two races could gradually live themselves out of their old relation to each other, and both come out better prepared for the new."

In other words, he wanted a system that would help blacks and whites overcome racism and resentment. One way to secure voting rights for freed slaves was to allow Confederate states back into the Union only if they allowed African Americans to vote.

Another of Lincoln's plans was to divide land that had been abandoned or seized into 40-acre plots. Former slaves would be given these plots to farm, and, after three years, they could buy the land. This would allow them to make a living for themselves. If this had happened, many newly freed slaves wouldn't have had to work for white landowners and remain in poverty.

And what of Confederate leaders? Lincoln didn't want to punish Confederate leaders, but he did want to "scare them off." He hoped that if Confederate leaders left the country, new leaders — both black and white — would emerge in the South. Instead, many Confederate leaders remained in power.

Perhaps most importantly, some historians believe Lincoln would have been able to work with Radical Republicans such as Edwin Stanton to form a strong and lasting plan for the South. Instead, President Johnson and the Radical Republicans never agreed. The constant bickering between Johnson and Stanton led to Johnson firing Stanton. In retaliation, the Radical Republicans brought charges against Johnson to remove him from office. After a trial, Johnson was acquitted by only one vote, and he remained president. All of this was a distraction from what was really important: rebuilding the South and securing equal rights for African Americans.

Other historians believe, however, that the nation wouldn't have been any better off if Lincoln had lived. He might not have been able to overcome resistance to his ideas. His plans for Reconstruction might not have been able to happen without placing a large military force in the South. And voters might have opposed funding such a huge military expense. Additionally, Lincoln would have been in office until only 1869. That wouldn't have given him much time to put his policies into place.

What do you think might have happened if Lincoln lived? Would the nation be in a better place today? We will never know. But one thing is certain: A single man, a single bullet, and a single second changed the course of history.

TIMELINE »»»»»»»»»»»»»»»»»»»»»»

Feb. 12, 1809: Abraham Lincoln is born in Kentucky

1830: The Lincoln family moves to Illinois

1834: Lincoln is elected to Illinois state legislature

1836: Lincoln receives his law license

May 10, 1838: John Wilkes Booth is born near Bel Air, Maryland

1842: Lincoln marries Mary Todd

1846: Lincoln is elected to U.S. House of Representatives

1855: Booth makes his first stage appearance as an actor in Shakespeare's *Richard III*

1859: Booth witnesses the execution of abolitionist John Brown

1860: Lincoln is elected president of the United States

1861: The Civil War begins at Fort Sumter, South Carolina

1862: The Lincolns' son Willie dies from typhoid

1863: Lincoln watches Booth perform in the play *The Marble Heart*

1863: The Emancipation Proclamation is issued

1864: Booth begins forming a plot to kidnap President Lincoln

March 1865: Booth's plan to kidnap President Lincoln fails

April 9, 1865: Confederate General Robert E. Lee surrenders to Union General Ulysses S. Grant

April 14, 1865: Booth shoots Lincoln at Ford's Theatre

April 15, 1865: Lincoln dies of his wounds; Andrew Johnson is sworn in as president

April 26, 1865: Booth is shot and killed by Sergeant Boston Corbett in Virginia

March 27, 1866: Johnson vetoes the Civil Rights Act, which protected rights of African Americans; Congress overrides his veto

Feb. 24, 1868: President Johnson is put on trial after firing Secretary of War Edwin P. Stanton

May 26, 1868: The Senate finds Johnson not guilty

1870: All former Confederate States have been readmitted into the Union

1876: Reconstruction officially ends

1964–65: The Civil Rights Act and Voting Rights Act finally give legal equality to African Americans

GLOSSARY

abolitionist—a person who worked to end slavery before the Civil War

accomplice—a person who helps another person do something illegal or wrong

conspirator—a person who is involved in a secret, illegal plan

emancipation—freeing someone from the control of another

inauguration—formal ceremony to swear a person into political office pillaging—stripping a place of its goods, often in a violent manner

procession—a number of people walking or driving along a route for a specific purpose

secession—withdrawal or separation from a country or group, often to form another country or group

smuggle—to take something in or out of a place secretly or illegally

territories—lands and waters under control of a specific nation, such as areas belonging to the United States that are not states

tyrant—someone who rules other people in a cruel or unjust way

SOURCE NOTES

Page 6, line 6: Steers, Edward Jr. *Blood on the Moon: The Assassination of Abraham Lincoln.* Lexington, Ky.: The University Press of Kentucky, 2001, p. 91.

Page 9, line 8: Holzer, Harold, Ed. *President Lincoln Assassinated!! The Firsthand Story of the Murder, Manhunt, Trial, and Mourning.* New York: Penguin Random House, 2014, p. 6.

Page 9, line 13: Booth, John Wilkes. *Right or Wrong, God Judge Me: The Writings of John Wilkes Booth.* Rhodehamel, John and Louise Taper, Eds. Urbana, Ill.: University of Illinois Press, 1997, p. 55.

Page 20, line 26: Holzer, Harold. *"What if Abraham Lincoln Had Lived?" CNN Politics. October 6, 2015. http://www.cnn.com/2016/10/06/politics/had-abraham-lincoln-lived-counterfactual/index.html*

Page 21, line 9: Carpenter, Francis Bicknell. *Six Months at the White House with Abraham Lincoln.* New York: Hurd and Houghton, 1866.; reprinted by Applewood Books in Bedford, Mass., pp 30-31.

Page 44, line 16: Axelrod, Alan. *Lincoln's Last Night: Abraham Lincoln, John Wilkes Booth, and the Last 36 Hours Before the Assassination.* New York: Penguin Group, 2005, p. 90.

Page 49, line 7: *Right or Wrong, God Judge Me: The Writings of John Wilkes Booth*, p. 154.

Page 50, line 7: *Blood on the Moon: The Assassination of Abraham Lincoln*, p. 204.

Page 56, line 11: Guelzo, Allen. "What if Abraham Lincoln Had Lived?" *The Washington Post*. 13 April 2015. October 2017. https://www.washingtonpost.com/posteverything/ wp/2015/04/13/ what-if-abraham-lincoln-had-lived/

Page 56, line 25: "What if Abraham Lincoln Had Lived?"

SELECT BIBLIOGRAPHY

Axelrod, Alan. *Lincoln's Last Night: Abraham Lincoln, John Wilkes Booth, and the Last 36 Hours Before the Assassination*. New York: Penguin Group, 2005.

Booth, John Wilkes. *Right or Wrong, God Judge Me: The Writings of John Wilkes Booth*. Rhodehamel, John and Louise Taper, Eds. Urbana, Ill.: University of Illinois Press, 1997.

Carpenter, Francis Bicknell. *Six Months at the White House with Abraham Lincoln*. New York: Hurd and Houghton, 1866.; reprinted by Applewood Books in Bedford, Mass.

Clarke, James W. *American Assassins: The Darker Side of Politics*. Princeton, N.J.: Princeton University Press, 1982.

Guelzo, Allen. "What if Abraham Lincoln Had Lived?" *The Washington Post*. 13 April 2015. October 2017. https://www.washingtonpost.com/posteverything/ wp/2015/04/13/what-if-abraham-lincoln-had-lived/

Hodes, Martha. *Mourning Lincoln*. New Haven, Conn.: Yale University Press, 2015.

Holzer, Harold, Ed. *President Lincoln Assassinated!! The Firsthand Story of the Murder, Manhunt, Trial, and Mourning*. New York: Penguin Random House, 2014.

Kauffman, Michael W. *American Brutus: John Wilkes Booth and the Lincoln Conspiracies*. New York: Random House, 2004.

Leonard, Elizabeth. *Lincoln's Avengers: Justice, Revenge, and Reunion After the Civil War*. New York: W.W. Norton & Company, 2004.

Lindop, Edmund. *Assassinations that Shook America*. New York: Franklin Watts, 1992.

Steers, Edward Jr. *Blood on the Moon: The Assassination of Abraham Lincoln*. Lexington, Ky.: The University Press of Kentucky, 2001.

Swanson, James L. and Weinberg, Daniel R. *Lincoln's Assassins: Their Trial and Execution*. Santa Fe, N.M.: Arena Editions, 2001.

"What if Abraham Lincoln Had Lived?" *CNN Politics*. 6 October 2015. October 2017. http://www. cnn.com/2016/10/06/politics/had-abraham-lincoln-lived-counterfactual/index.html

ADDITIONAL RESOURCES

READ MORE

Brown, Don. *He Has Shot the President!: April 14, 1865: The Day John Wilkes Booth Killed President Lincoln*. New York: Roaring Book Press, 2014.

Gunderson, Jessica. *The Wound Is Mortal: The Story of the Assassination of Abraham Lincoln*. North Mankato, Minn: Capstone Press, 2016.

Langston-George, Rebecca. *The Booth Brothers: Drama, Fame, and the Death of President Lincoln*. North Mankato, Minn: Capstone Press, 2018.

INTERNET SITES

Use FactHound to find Internet sites related to this book.

Visit www.facthound.com

Just type in 9780756557164 and go.

INDEX

ABOUT THE AUTHOR

JESSICA GUNDERSON

grew up in the small town of Washburn, North Dakota. She has a bachelor's degree from the University of North Dakota and an MFA in Creative Writing from Minnesota State University, Mankato. She has written more than seventy-five books for young readers. An avid enthusiast of Civil War history and Abraham Lincoln, she is the author of *The Election of 1860: A Nation Divides on the Eve of War* and *The Wound is Mortal: The Story of the Assassination of Abraham Lincoln*. She currently lives in Madison, Wisconsin, with her husband and cat.

PHOTO CREDITS